Clothed With Kindness

Coloring with Kindness

When you are dressed nice you feel nice and in that moment you say "I'm cute today or handsome". Words are the same way, understanding you have to be mindful of what to say to yourself and others. Because words are weighty and can either dress you up or like the wrong outfit choice impact your confidence. In this coloring book we will address how to engage hostile interactions with Kind words to establish a Kind Culture. Youth across this country are cutting themselves and committing suicide because of bullying. Kindness is an approach to bullying that considers how others feel, using your words positively to build people up. Even the most active parents who pay attention to the details need help. Support is necessary from multiple sources to approach the Culture that lends itself to ridicule and cruelty. When our youth use Kind words with peers and friends we can stop bullying before it gets started.

Words like the wind seem to pass but do words really disappear. Across this country there are young people and adults who struggle beyond what was done. Trying to overcome the hurtful words that were said during that time.

What word would best describe this outfit and why?

1. What clothing item stood out to you the most?

2. Why did that clothing item stick out to you?

3. Who picked their clothing item because you've worn that item in the past?

When we have a favorite jacket or sweater we wear it for comfort or because it feels good. In the same way we use words that we are most comfortable with, whether they are good or not so good.

What word would you use to describe how the person might feel in this picture?

1. Why did you choose that particular word?

2. Please define the meaning of the word you chose.

3. Describe a time when you've felt the same way as the word you chose?

Describe the last time you were concerned, upset or sad about something.

1. What situation upsets you the most?

2. What thoughts or circumstances cause you to be concerned or upset about things?

3. What words could be used that would make you sad?

For a lot of us when we are concerned, upset or sad we read a book, play outside or we use technology during those times.

1. What's your favorite book, subject or show on YouTube?

2. What do you download the most when you have spare time?

3. How do you feel when you watch this show or play a particular game?

What does the word influence mean to you?

1. What food item do you eat because your mom or dad exposed you to it?

2. What brand name or designer clothing do you prefer or like the most?

3. How do you feel when you wear this brand of clothing?

We are impacted by the people we live with and without even being conscious we like things because they were presented to us by the people around us.

We wash our hands because germs exist so being clean is important. How much more should we choose to watch (or wash) our words every day.

Someone may have said to you that you are not cute or that you don't have value but like an outfit that's not yours. Refuse to accept or wear those words and understand you are beautiful and you have great value.

We wear jackets when it's cold outside to protect us from cold weather and to prevent getting a cold or the flu.

1.   What is the most beautiful quality about your personality?

2. Name a person you know that has a beautiful personality.

3. Give an example of what makes their personality so great.

When the sign says Kindness you expect Kindness. Our words are a sign of what people will expect to receive from us. So use Kind words to build people up and not tear them down.

Think about your favorite outfit, doesn't it make you smile. Your words can cause people to frown or smile so be mindful to be Kind with your words.

1.   Describe the last time you were so happy that you couldn't stop smiling.

2. What made that time so special for you?

3. Describe a time that you made someone feel special and what you did that day?

Words are powerful and when you say things like "Your reading in class was great today or you were on point with your answers in class today". You build a bond with classmates to become friends.

Tell us about a time you wore something or tried something on that was too big for you or that you didn't like?

1. What was the clothing item?

2. How did it look on you or why didn't you like it ?

3. Did you want to wear it after trying it on or looking at it more closely?

Like a pop up Ad on YouTube that disturbs what you're watching. You can always reject negative words like "Ugly, stupid , fat, lame, and other insulting terms". Because those words do not belong to you so refuse to be interested in those words.

The words that describe you are beautiful, valuable, creative, Kind, caring, nice. Let's test this out and use some of these words to describe a peer or classmate.

When you use Kind words you create acceptance in your home, school and community. Always consider your words like picking out what coat to wear when it's cold outside.

When you come to school you have expectations for the staff and Teachers to be helpful and Kind. That expectation makes sense but students also help to Create A Kind Culture Through Kind words.

Like your favorite Jean jacket, your words create a
cozy and Kind environment for others.

Our commitment as parents, teachers, counselors
and staff is to clothe you with words that allow you to be
the best version of yourself that you can be.

We are not too busy to hear what's on your mind.
Never feel like you can't ask your parents, teacher or staff
questions about how you feel or something that was
said.

Mom and Dad working together to stop Bullying

Cultivating creativity & family values through coloring
www.richiepatterson.com

#THISISTHEKINDNESS #COLORINGWITHKINDNESS

It takes a group effort to stop bullying
Kindness is an approach not a reaction to bullying

Cultivating creativity & family values through coloring
www.richiepatterson.com

#THISISTHEKINDNESS #COLORINGWITHKINDNESS

Available for Workshops, Speaking Engagements, Open Forums, Counseling Sessions And More

Pastor Richie Patterson III
8225 Allen Rd #1018
Allen Park, MI 48101
248.372.9500
www.richiepatterson.com

#THISISTHEKINDNESS
#COLORINGWITHKINDNESS

THIS IS THE KINDNESS
Kindness
defeats
Bullying
Cultivating creativity moving
beyond negativity
#THISISTHEKINDNESS #COLORINGWITHKINDNESS